Liebe ist...
Dich
zu heiraten
zum Mond
und zurück
Dich sooo
Für
meinen
allerliebsten
Schatz
Mein
Herzerl
Gruß vom
Oktoberfest
2009

Marden Smith · Claudia Steiner

Oktoberfest!

Ich danke meinem tollen Assistenten Kilian, all den Organisatoren, Verantwortlichen, Wirten und Fahrgeschäftsbesitzern, die dieses Projekt ermöglicht haben, meinen Agentinnen Terri Manduca und Elke Froschauer, meinem Buchagenten Kai Gathemann sowie all den Oktoberfest-Besuchern, die gerne für mich posiert haben.

Thanks to my wonderful assistant Kilian, all the officials, tent and ride owners which helped to make this project possible, my agents Terri Manduca and Elke Froschauer, my book agent Kai Gathemann, and all the Oktoberfest visitors which happily posed for me.

Marden Smith

Marden Smith (Fotos) · Claudia Steiner (Text)

Oktoberfest!

Trachten, Bier und Achterbahnen

Dirndls, beer and rollercoasters

Ins Englische übertragen
von Jonathan Spink

terra magica

Es begann mit einer Märchenhochzeit …

Es war einmal eine fünf Tage dauernde Feier vor den Toren Münchens: Am 12. Oktober 1810 heiratete der bayerische Kronprinz Ludwig, der spätere König Ludwig I., die 18-jährige Prinzessin Therese von Sachsen-Hildburghausen. In der ganzen Stadt gab es ein Fest für die Bürger mit einer Parade der Schützen der Nationalgarde, Musik, Essen und Trinken. Und weil die Feierlichkeiten mit einem Pferderennen auf einer Wiese vor den Toren der Stadt, die zu Ehren der Braut »Theresienwiese« genannt wurde, zu Ende gingen, heißt das Oktoberfest bei den Münchnern auch heute noch »Wiesn«.

Da das Pferderennen beim Volk gut ankam, wurde es ein Jahr später wiederholt. 1811 wurde erstmals auch das Landwirtschaftsfest veranstaltet – es findet heute noch alle vier Jahre auf dem südlichen Teil der 42 Hektar großen Theresienwiese statt: Landwirte zeigen dort ihre Produkte, Züchter ihr schönstes Vieh und Landmaschinenhersteller die neuesten Geräte und Fahrzeuge.

Von da ab wurde auf der Theresienwiese jedes Jahr gefeiert: Hendl- und Ochsenbratereien gab es zunächst nicht, sondern nur ein paar Marktfrauen, die zum Beispiel Zwetschgen aus dem eigenen Garten verkauften. Auch die Unterhaltung war mit Kegelbahnen, Schaukeln und Losständen noch recht bescheiden. 1880 hielt das elektrische Licht auf der

It began with a fairytale wedding …

Once upon a time, a party was held outside the gates of Munich that lasted for five days: on October 12, 1810, Bavarian Crown Prince Ludwig, who was later crowned King Ludwig I, married 18-year-old Princess Therese von Sachsen-Hildburghausen. This party was held throughout the whole city for all of Munich's citizens, and included a parade with the riflemen of the National Guard, music, eating and drinking. And because the celebrations concluded with a horse race on the meadow outside the city's gates, which was named "Theresienwiese" in honour of the bride, today's inhabitants of Munich still refer to the Oktoberfest as the "Wiesn" ("Wiese" means "meadow" in German).

The horse race was repeated a year later thanks to the popularity it encountered among the populace. The agricultural festival was also staged in 1811 – it is still held today every four years on the southern part of the 42-hectare Theresienwiese: farmers display their products, breeders their best livestock, and agricultural machinery manufacturers the latest equipment and vehicles.

From then on, festivities were held every year on the Theresienwiese: at the start, there was no roast chicken or ox, instead simply a few market women selling, for example, plums from their own gardens. Entertainment was also still very modest, compris-

Blick auf die Theresienwiese, den Olympiaturm und die Paulskirche
View of the Theresienwiese, the Olympic Tower and the Paulskirche

ROTOR
ROTOR
Peaches
Cocktailbar
CAIPIRINHA

Wiesn Einzug. Einer der klügsten Köpfe Deutschlands verdingte sich übrigens in jungen Jahren als Glühbirnenschrauber im Schottenhamel auf der Wiesn: Albert Einstein. 1896 wurden dann die ersten großen Bierburgen errichtet. Wegen Cholera, Kriegen und Epidemien fiel das Oktoberfest insgesamt 24 Mal aus. Während der Wirtschaftskrise in den 1920er-Jahren fand die Wiesn zwar statt, allerdings mussten die Besucher 1922 ganze 50 Mark für eine Maß und sogar 500 Mark für ein Hendl hinblättern.

Inzwischen ist das Münchner Oktoberfest ein bayerischer Exportschlager – es gibt Kopien des Volksfestes in den USA, Kanada, Brasilien und vielen anderen Ländern. Die echte Wiesn aber, die gibt es nur in München. Und dazu gehören nicht nur Lebkuchenherzen und Lederhosen, Bier und Brathendl, sondern auch die traditionellen Umzüge. Am ersten Wiesn-Samstag ziehen die Festwirte und Braue-

ing bowling alleys, swings and lottery stands. Electric illumination was first introduced to the Oktoberfest in 1880. Incidentally, one of Germany's greatest minds, as a young man, took a job installing light bulbs in the Schottenhamel tent at the Oktoberfest: Albert Einstein. The first large beer tents were then set up in 1896. The Oktoberfest was cancelled on a total of 24 occasions due to cholera, wars and epidemics. Although the Oktoberfest was held during the economic crisis of the 1920s, visitors in 1922 were required to pay no less than 50 marks for a litre of beer, and even as much as 500 marks for a roast chicken.

The Munich Oktoberfest has meanwhile become a Bavarian export hit – there are even copies of the Oktoberfest held in the USA, Canada, Brazil and many other countries. But the genuine Oktoberfest takes place only in Munich. And the real Oktoberfest includes not only gingerbread hearts and lederhosen, beer, and roast chicken, but also the traditional parades. On the first Saturday of the Oktoberfest, the beer-tent landlords and breweries parade their horses and carts, which are festooned with flowers and garlands, through the inner city all the way to the Theresienwiese. The people of Munich line the streets, cheering the waitresses swinging beer mugs on the carriages. Shortly later, these waitresses will be serving them their first, fresh litres of beer. This parade was held for the first time in 1887.

reien auf blumen- und girlandengeschmückten Prachtgespannen durch die Innenstadt bis zur Theresienwiese. Die Münchner stehen am Straßenrand und jubeln den bierkrugschwenkenden Kellnerinnen auf den Kutschen zu, die ihnen kurze Zeit später die erste, frische Maß servieren. Dieser Umzug fand 1887 zum ersten Mal statt.

Einen Tag später, am ersten Wiesn-Sonntag, ziehen die »Trachtler« durch die Innenstadt. Diese Parade fand erstmals 1835 anlässlich der Silberhochzeit von König Ludwig I. und Therese von Bayern statt. Heute nehmen an dem Umzug mehrere Tausend Sport- und Gebirgsschützen, Musikkapellen, Trachtengruppen, Spielmannszüge, Fahnenschwinger, aufgeputzte Braurösser, Festwägen und Kutschen teil. Der Zug wird traditionell hoch zu Ross vom Münchner Kindl angeführt. Das ist kein Kind, sondern eine junge Frau, die meist aus einer Münchner Kaufmanns- oder Brauereifamilie stammt und die die Stadt als »Botschafterin« repräsentiert. Die Zuschauer entlang der Parade bestaunen die prunkvollen Trachten, denn Tracht ist wieder »in«. Während vor 25 Jahren Münchner Teenagerinnen nur unter Strafandrohungen der Eltern ihr Dirndl angezogen haben, tragen heute

Performers in traditional Bavarian costume parade through the inner city a day later, on the first Sunday of the Oktoberfest. This parade was held for the first time in 1835, on the occasion of the silver wedding anniversary of King Ludwig I and Therese of Bavaria. Today, several thousands of sports and mountain marksmen, music bands, groups dressed in traditional Bavarian costume, bandsmen, flag-throwers, decorated dray-horses, festive carriages and coaches participate in the parade. The parade is traditionally led by the Munich "Kindl" on horseback (in Bavarian-German dialect literally: "little child"). But the "Kindl" is not a child, but rather a young woman, mostly from one of Munich's business or brewery families, who represents the city as an "ambassador". Onlookers along the route of the parade admire the ornate, traditional Bavarian costumes. In the meantime, such costumes are fashionable once again. Whereas, 25 years ago, teenage girls from Munich would have donned traditional Bavarian dresses only under the threat of punishment from their parents, young people today again enjoy wearing such fetching costumes. In any case, half of Munich can be seen wearing traditional Bavarian dresses or leder-

Jugendliche wieder gerne eine kesse Tracht. Überhaupt läuft während der Wiesn halb München in Dirndl und Lederhose herum, sogar Crews der Lufthansa tauschen auf ausgewählten Strecken das dunkelblaue Kostüm gegen ein fesches blaues Dirndl mit gelber Schürze.
Die größte Herausforderung des Oktoberfestes ist und bleibt jedoch die Organisation: Die Polizei zeigt Präsenz und in den Zelten werden Raufbolde innerhalb von Sekunden von Ordnern vor die Tür gesetzt. In den U-Bahnen gibt es »Ansager«, die die Massen antreiben (»Geh ma, geh ma«) und mit bayerischem Humor in die Bierzelte lotsen. Insgesamt arbeiten jährlich rund 12.000 Menschen auf der Wiesn. Die Theresienwiese selbst ist wie eine Stadt in der Stadt mit Polizei- und Krankenstation, Gepäckaufbewahrung, einer Post und sogar einer Kinderfundstelle, denn immer wieder gehen Kinder in dem Trubel verloren. Und dann gibt es natürlich auch ein richtiges Fundbüro, in dem sich während der Wiesn so einiges ansammelt: Hunderte Handys, Schlüssel, Geldbörsen, Jacken, Taschen, Gebisse, Hörgeräte, aber auch Laptops, Krücken und Eheringe …
Die Wiesn ist echte Tradition, aber auch ein gutes Geschäft. Der Wirtschaftswert des Oktoberfestes

hosen during the Oktoberfest. Even Lufthansa air hostesses swap their dark uniforms for a chic blue Bavarian dress topped off with a yellow pinafore on certain routes.
The greatest challenge presented by the Oktoberfest, however, is and remains organisation: the police are out in force, and bouncers are quick to eject rowdies from the tents. In subway stations, announcers drive the masses forward ("let's go! let's go!"), steering them towards the beer tents with Bavarian humour. Every year, the Oktoberfest employs a total of around 12,000 people. The Theresienwiese itself is like a city within a city with its own police and first aid stations, luggage deposit, a post office, and even a centre for lost children (children are forever getting lost in the crowd). Then, of course, there is also a real lost property office where all sorts of objects pile up during the Oktoberfest: hundreds of mobile telephones, keys, wallets, jackets, bags, false teeth, hearing aids, as well as laptops, crutches, and wedding rings …
The Oktoberfest is not only a genuine tradition, but also good business. The economic value of the Oktoberfest amounts to around €830 million; not only breweries and travel businesses, but also hotels, taxis, restaurants and businesses benefit from

beträgt rund 830 Millionen Euro; nicht nur Brauereien und Fahrgeschäfte, auch Hotels, Taxis, Restaurants und Geschäfte profitieren von dem Rummel mitten in der Stadt. Jedes Jahr bewerben sich mehr als 1.400 Schausteller, Marktkaufleute und Gastronomiebetriebe, um einen der begehrten Plätze auf der Theresienwiese, gut 600 werden zugelassen. Wer einen Tisch oder eine Box in den Zelten haben möchte, muss sich zwar nicht bewerben, aber Monate im Voraus buchen. Denn die Tische sind nicht nur bei Münchner Firmen, die Mitarbeiter und Kunden aufs Oktoberfest einladen, beliebt, sondern auch bei Promis aus dem In- und Ausland. Wer war nicht schon alles zu Besuch: Schauspieler und Entertainer Johannes Heesters stemmt auch mit über 100 noch die Maß, Model Marcus Schenkenberg trug bei seinem Besuch wie alle anderen Lederhose und ließ die Frauenherzen schneller schlagen und auch Hotelerbin Paris Hilton posierte schon für die Fotografen – im goldenen Dirndl. Wenn schon, denn schon!

the hustle and bustle in the city centre. Each year, more than 1,400 exhibitors, market stallholders and gastronomic businesses apply for the sought-after places at the Oktoberfest. A good 600 receive permits. Although individuals or companies seeking a table or a box in the tents are not required to submit applications, bookings nevertheless need to be made months in advance. This is because the tables are not only popular with Munich companies that invite staff and customers to the Oktoberfest, but also with celebs from both Germany and abroad. And who has not been to the Oktoberfest? Actor and entertainer Johannes Heesters, who is over 100 years old in the meantime, still likes to raise a litre jug of beer. Like everyone else, model Marcus Schenkenberg wore lederhosen when he made his visit, much to the delight of the ladies, and hotel heiress Paris Hilton has posed in the past for the photographers – wearing a golden traditional Bavarian dress. Something worth doing, is worth doing well.

Am ersten Wiesn-Wochenende ziehen die Wirte und Tausende Trachtler aus dem In- und Ausland durch die Stadt.
On the first Oktoberfest weekend, beer-tent landlords and thousands of people, who come from both Germany and abroad to don traditional costume, parade through the city.

Der Münchner Oberbürgermeister Christian Ude (rechts) beim Trachtenumzug
The Lord Mayor of Munich, Christian Ude (right), during the parade of traditional costumes

KAFFEE HAG

Trachtler und geschmückte Festwagen ziehen an der Feldherrnhalle und der Theatinerkirche vorbei.
Decorated drays and performers in traditional costume pass the Feldherrnhalle and Theatinerkirche.

SZ-
BayWa

Braurösser beim Einzug auf die Wiesn
Dray-horses at the entry to the Oktoberfest grounds

PAULANER
PAULANER

LÖWEN
LÖWENBRÄU
Zimmermann
Zimmermann
Pschorr

Lichtenegger's
Mandeln

FREEFALL
SHOP

SCHOTTENHAMEL
SPATENBRÄU
SCHOTTENHAMEL

Alphornbläser
vor der Bavaria
Alphorn players in
front of the statue
of Bavaria

PAULANER

SKATER
Folgender Personenkreis
Personen, die an Wirbelsäulen-oder
die deswegen
sowie Herz-u. Kreislaufkr
Kinder unter 10 Jahren, bzw.
Personen, die auf Grund ihres
Sicherheitsbügel nicht sicher
Betrunkene oder berauschte
Das Hinauslehnen aus der
das Mitnehme
und anderen spitzen
Während der
und sich an
der Kopf ist an die
Den Anordnungen
geschlos
thochdruck leid
mitfahren.
m Körpergröße,
durch die vorhandene
n nicht mitfahren.
Podium nicht betreten.
Beinen, das Rauchen,
Gläsern
nden ist verboten.
itzenbleiben
festhalten,
er anzulehnen.
olge zu leisten.
SKATER

HB
Susi

Von Commissari und Bierkontrolleuren

Warum reist ein Australier um die ganze Welt, um mühsam das Trinklied »Oans, zwoa, gsuffa« zu lernen? Warum rücken Italiener mit Wohnmobilen an, um mit Tausenden Nichtitalienern lauthals »Azzurro« zu singen? Und warum lassen junge Frauen aus Tokio ihr Designer-Outfit im Schrank hängen, um sich eine Schürze umzubinden?

Jahr für Jahr erlebt München von Ende September bis Anfang Oktober für rund zwei Wochen die fünfte Jahreszeit und damit den Ausnahmezustand. In den Bierzelten lassen sich Tausende vom Kapellmeister auf die Bänke treiben und schmettern Wiesn-Hits wie »Hey Baby«, während junge Frauen, die die Wirkung des Biers unterschätzt haben, lassoartig ihre Büstenhalter über dem Kopf schwingen. Zwar kommen 72 Prozent der Wiesn-Besucher aus Bayern und neun Prozent aus den übrigen Bundesländern, der Rest reist jedoch zum größten Volksfest der Welt aus dem Ausland an: aus Österreich, der Schweiz, Frankreich, Großbritannien, den USA, Australien, Neuseeland, Fernost – und natürlich aus Italien.

Bei den Italienern ist das »Festa di Ottobre« oder »Festa della Birra« besonders beliebt. Wenn am mittleren Wiesn-Wochenende traditionell die Italiener anrücken, verwandelt sich München beinahe in eine norditalienische Metropole. Das Radio sen-

Commissari and beer inspectors

Why does an Australian travel all the way round the world to struggle to learn the words to the drinking song "Oans, zwoa, gsuffa" ("One, two, three and bottoms up!" – a very well-known, traditional Munich tavern song)? Why do Italians with caravans come to sing "Azzurro" at the top of their voices with thousands of non-Italians? And why do young women from Tokyo leave their designer outfits hanging in their wardrobes to don traditional Bavarian dress?

Each year, for a two-week period from the end of September until the beginning of October, Munich experiences its fifth season, and, with it, a departure from everyday life. In the beer tents, thousands dance on benches to the lead of the bandmasters, and belt out Oktoberfest hits such as "Hey Baby", while young women, who have underestimated the impact of the beer, swing their bras over their heads like lassoes. Although 72 percent of Oktoberfest visitors come from Bavaria, and 9 percent from other parts of Germany, the rest of the people assembling for the world's largest popular festival hail from abroad: from Austria, Switzerland, France, Great Britain, the USA, Australia, New Zealand, the Far East – and, of course, Italy.

The "Festa di Ottobre" or "Festa della Birra" is particularly popular among Italians. Munich almost

det Verkehrshinweise auf Italienisch, um die Fahrer aus Milano, Roma und Firenze auf freie Wohnwagenparkplätze zu lotsen. Jeden Morgen sitzen dann verknitterte »Ragazzi« vor ihrem Wohnmobil und beginnen den Tag so, wie die Nacht zuvor geendet hat: mit Bier. Auf der Wiesn gehen »Commissari« zusammen mit deutschen Polizisten auf Streife, damit es nicht zu Verständigungsproblemen kommt.

Wenn die Bierzelte wegen Überfüllung geschlossen werden, ist die Enttäuschung bei den weit gereisten Bierfans groß. Dann drängeln sich Hunderte vor den Zelteingängen und versuchen, die Ordner mit Charme oder Dekolleté doch noch zum Einlass zu überreden. Zwar gibt es auf dem Oktoberfest insgesamt rund 100.000 Sitzplätze – das größte Zelt fasst um die 10.000 Menschen –, aber die sind oft schon kurz nach Eröffnung bis auf den allerletzten Platz besetzt.

Gaudi bedeutet auf dem Oktoberfest übrigens nicht gleich Gaudi. Jedes der 14 Großzelte hat nicht nur sein eigenes Bier, sondern auch seine eigene Kundschaft und seine eigene, ganz besondere Stimmung. Das Festzelt der Familie Schottenhamel zum Beispiel steht schon seit 1867 auf der Wiesn und ist

turns into a north-Italian metropolis when the Italians traditionally arrive on the mid-Oktoberfest weekend. The radio issues traffic instructions in Italian to steer motorists from Milan, Rome and Florence in the direction of free caravan spaces. Then, every morning, crumpled "ragazzi" can be seen sitting outside their caravans, starting the day the same way the previous night ended: with beer. To avoid communication problems, "commissari" patrol together with the German police around the Oktoberfest grounds.

Disappointment is considerable among beer fans who have travelled from far and wide if the beer tents are closed due to overfilling. Then hundreds crowd around the tent entrances, attempting to persuade the doorkeepers to admit them nevertheless, while employing charm or a plunging neckline. Although the Oktoberfest beer tents seat around 100,000 guests in total – the largest tent can accommodate around 10,000 people – they are frequently filled to the very last seat almost as soon as the tents open.

By the way, fun at the Oktoberfest does not mean that the fun is the same everywhere. Each of the 14 major tents not only has its own beer, but also its

damit das älteste Festzelt. Vor allem bei den jungen Münchnern ist es »angesagt«. Das weltberühmte Hofbräu-Festzelt ist bei ausländischen Besuchern sehr beliebt. Das Augustiner gilt dagegen als Münchner Traditionszelt. Das Löwenbräu-Zelt, über dessen Eingang ein 4,5 Meter hoher Löwe wacht und auch brüllt, ist wiederum das Zelt der »Löwen«, der Fußballfans des TSV 1860 München, und im hippen Hippodrom soll man besonders gut flirten können.

Schon etwa zwei Monate vor Beginn des Oktoberfestes fängt auf der Theresienwiese die »Vor-Wiesn« an. Dann arbeiten Hunderte Bauarbeiter, Zimmerleute, Elektriker und Dekorateure daran, das Volksfest aufzubauen. Das bedeutet echte Vorfreude für viele Einheimische: Sie schauen alle paar Tage vorbei, um zu sehen, wie weit die Arbeiten schon gediehen sind. Anschließend setzen sie sich in eine der Kantinen, die eigentlich für die Arbeiter gedacht sind, um sich eine erste Maß zu genehmigen.

Eröffnet wird die Wiesn traditionell am ersten Samstag um Punkt 12 Uhr mittags vom Münchner

own clientele, and its own, quite unique atmosphere. The Schottenhamel family's beer tent, for instance, has been at the Oktoberfest since as early as 1867, making it the oldest beer tent. It is "the place to be", particularly among Munich's young. The world-famous Hofbräu beer tent is especially popular among foreign visitors. The Augustiner, by contrast, is regarded as the traditional Munich beer tent. The Löwenbräu tent, in its turn, which boasts a 4.5-meter-high lion above its entrance that also growls, is the tent of the "Löwen" (in German this means "lions"), the football fans of TSV 1860 München. The hip "Hippodrom" is also said to be a particularly good place to flirt.

From as early as about two months before the Oktoberfest's start, the "pre-Oktoberfest" gets underway on the Theresienwiese. This is the time when hundreds of construction workers, carpenters, electricians and decorators construct the festival. For many local people, this constitutes a genuine pleasure in anticipation: they stop by every few days to see how far work has progressed. They then go and

Oberbürgermeister im Schottenhamel-Zelt. Die Zeitungen spekulieren schon Tage im Voraus, wie viele Schläge der Stadtvater dieses Mal brauchen wird, bis der erste, goldgelbe Gerstensaft aus dem Holzfass fließt. Die beste Leistung vollbrachte Christian Ude 2005, 2008 und 2009 mit nur jeweils zwei Schlägen, den Negativrekord stellte 1950 Thomas Wimmer mit ganzen 19 Schlägen auf. »O'zapft is!«, verkündet der Politiker dann vor der versammelten Presse und wünscht eine »friedliche Wiesn«. Die erste Maß geht traditionell an den bayerischen Ministerpräsidenten. Dann werden zwölf Böllerschüsse abgegeben. Nun dürfen auch die anderen Wirte ausschenken. Bedienungen sprinten dann durch die Zelte und Biergärten. Sie tragen – Leistungssportlern gleich – Lederbandagen an den Handgelenken und balancieren zehn Bierkrüge und mehr von Tisch zu Tisch. In der Luft liegt der Geruch von knusprigen »Hendln« und der süße Duft von gebrannten Mandeln. In den kommenden zwei

sit in one of the canteens, which are actually intended for the workers, to enjoy their first litre of beer.

The Lord Mayor of Munich traditionally opens the Oktoberfest on the first Saturday, punctually at midday, in the Schottenhamel tent. Days in advance, newspapers speculate how many strikes with the mallet the Lord Mayor will require this year before the first, golden-yellow beer flows from the wooden barrel. Christian Ude was the best performer, who needed only two blows in 2005, 2008 and 2009, whereas the worst record was set by Thomas Wimmer in 1950 with a total of no fewer than 19 strikes. The politician then announces "O'zapft is!" (in Bavarian dialect this means: "the beer is tapped!") to the gathered press, and wishes everyone a "peaceful Oktoberfest". The first litre is then traditionally passed to the Prime Minister of Bavaria. Twelve gun salutes are fired. Only then are the other landlords permitted to start to serve their beer. Waiters sprint through the tents and beer gardens. They wear leather bandages around their wrists like sportsmen, balancing ten beer mugs or more as they make their way from table to table. The smell of crispy roast chicken wafts through the air, along with the sweet aroma of roast almonds. Over the course of the next two weeks, around six million visitors will drink more than six million litres of beer, consume almost a half a million roast chickens, more than 100,000 pairs of bratwurst, and no fewer than one hundred oxen.

Wochen trinken die rund sechs Millionen Besucher dann mehr als sechs Millionen Liter Bier, verspeisen fast eine halbe Million Brathendl, mehr als 100.000 Paar Bratwürstl und gut 100 Ochsen.

Viele der Profibedienungen arbeiten Jahr für Jahr auf der Wiesn, aus Tradition, aber auch weil sie in den zwei Wochen deutlich mehr verdienen als in derselben Zeit in ihrem eigentlichen Job. Die eine oder andere nimmt sich sogar extra Urlaub, um auf dem Oktoberfest arbeiten zu können. Sogar ein katholischer Pfarrer aus München tauscht die Priesterkluft gegen die »Krachlederne« ein und arbeitet als Ober – allerdings nicht, um seine Urlaubskasse aufzubessern, sondern für einen guten Zweck, versteht sich.

Ausgeschenkt wird übrigens nur Münchner Bier. Jede Brauerei stellt dafür ein eigenes Wiesn-Bier her. Es schmeckt etwas süßer und malziger. Der Grund: Oktoberfestbiere haben eine Stammwürze von gut 13,5 Prozent und einen höheren Alkoholgehalt, nämlich um die 5,8 Prozent. Gebraut wird der Gerstensaft natürlich nach dem Bayerischen Reinheitsgebot vom 23. April 1516. Es besagt, dass zur Herstellung von Bier nur Gerste, Hopfen und Wasser verwendet werden dürfen. Hefe wurde damals noch nicht erwähnt, da man noch nicht wusste, dass sie eine Voraussetzung für die Gärung ist.

Ein Politikum ist jedes Jahr der Bierpreis. Denn die Maß wird von Jahr zu Jahr teurer. »Oktoberfest-Wirte schlimmer als Ölkonzerne«, titelte einst die

Many of the professional waiters and waitresses work every year at the Oktoberfest, not only as a matter of tradition, but also because they can earn significantly more during these two weeks than they would during the same period in their own jobs. Some take extra vacation to be able to work at the Oktoberfest. There is even a Catholic priest from Munich who exchanges his priest's robes for lederhosen, and works as a waiter – not, however, to top up his vacation savings, but for a good cause, of course.

Only Munich beer is served, by the way. Each brewery brews its own Oktoberfest beer especially for the occasion. Its taste is a little sweeter and maltier than normal beer. This is because Oktoberfest beers have an original gravity of a good 13.5 percent, and a higher alcohol content of about 5.8 percent. The beer is brewed according to the Bavarian Beer Purity Act of April 23, 1516, of course. The act stipulates that beer is manufactured from only barley,

»Süddeutsche Zeitung« und verglich Bier- und Spritpreise der vergangenen Jahrzehnte. »Aussis«, »Kiwis« und »Amis« stört das jedoch wenig. Wer um die ganze Welt zur »Biggest Beer Party« anreist, erwartet eine Mordsgaudi und keine Billigparty. Ganz so dramatisch wie oft beschrieben ist der Bierpreis auf der Wiesn dann aber auch wieder nicht – zahlt man doch schon in vielen Münchner Kneipen um die 3,50 Euro für die Halbe – ohne Live-Musik und ohne Wiesn-Spektakel.

Damit jeder Gast zumindest das im Glas hat, was er bezahlt, gehen Kontrolleure des Vereins gegen betrügerisches Einschenken e.V., kurz VGBE, durch die Zelte und messen genau nach. Der Eichstrich steht 16,5 Zentimeter über dem Boden des Maßkrugs. Offiziell erlaubt ist ein minimaler Unterschank. Wenn mindestens 15 Zentimeter Bier gemessen werden können, ist alles im »goldgelben Bereich«. Ob aus Versehen oder mit Absicht – Unterschank ist ein gutes Geschäft für die Wirte: Laut

hops and water. Brewer's yeast was not yet mentioned at this time because the fact that it is required for fermentation was still unknown.

The price of beer is a political issue every year. This is because it becomes ever more expensive with every passing year. "Oktoberfest landlords worse than oil companies", once appeared as a headline in the "Süddeutsche Zeitung", before the newspaper went on to compare beer and petrol prices over recent decades. This does little to deter the "Aussies", "Kiwis", and "Yanks", however. Oktoberfest visitors who have travelled all the way round the world to the "Biggest Beer Party", arrive in the expectation of having great fun, and not a party on the cheap. On the other hand, however, the price of beer at the Oktoberfest is not quite as dramatically high as is often depicted: it should be recalled that a half a litre of beer costs around €3.50 in many of Munich's bars – and this price does not include live music and the Oktoberfest spectacle.

Inspectors from the Association against Fraudulent Beer-Pouring make their way through the tents, performing precise measurements to ensure that all guests receive the quantity of beer for which they have paid. The line measure is 16.5 centimetres above the bottom of the litre mug. A minimal degree of under-pouring is officially permitted. This quantity is said to be within the "gold-yellow range" if at least 15 centimetres of beer can be measured. Whether by accident or intentionally, under-pouring is good business for the landlords:

VGBE beschert bereits 0,1 Liter weniger im Krug den Wiesn-Wirten bei sechs Millionen verkaufter Maß einen Gewinn von ca. 4,5 Millionen Euro.

Doch spätestens nach der zweiten Maß schaut niemand mehr so genau auf den Eichstrich. Dann stehen Münchnerinnen neben Burschen aus Manchester und Mailänder neben Mannheimerinnen auf den Bänken. Beim Schunkeln kommen sich vor Kurzem noch Unbekannte schnell näher. Doch ist das »Madl«, das einem lächelnd zuprostet, noch zu haben oder fängt man sich womöglich vom Freund oder Ehemann eine »Watschn« ein? Die Schleife der Dirndlschürze verrät es – zumindest theoretisch: Trägt die Dame die Schleife auf der linken Seite, ist sie ungebunden, also »anbandeln« erwünscht! Schleife rechts bedeutet verheiratet, Schleife vorne in der Mitte heißt, man hat es mit einer Jungfrau zu tun. Schleife hinten geschnürt bedeutet verwitwet – oder dass die Dame dort kellnert. Auf diese Tradition kann man sich heute allerdings nicht

according to the Association against Fraudulent Beer-Pouring, a quantity of 0.1 litres per mug of under-pouring generates a profit of around €4.5 million for the Oktoberfest landlords, on the basis of six million litres sold in total.

By the second litre at the latest, however, customers no longer care quite as much about the line measure. By this time, women from Munich will be standing on the benches next to lads from Manchester, and visitors from Milan can be found alongside citizens of Mannheim. People who only a short time previously had been complete strangers rapidly get to know each other as the crowds sway to the music. Is the girl ("Madl") who smiles as she says "Cheers!", available, however, or might a slap on the face ("Watschn") from her boyfriend or husband be the more likely outcome? The bow on her traditional Bavarian dress should provide some clue – at least in theory: if the lady has tied the bow on the left side, she is uncommitted, in other words, she should welcome attempts to get to know her better. A bow on the right-hand side signifies that she is married, and a bow at the front in the middle signifies that she is a virgin. A bow tied at the back means that the lady is a widow – or that she is working there as a waitress. It is no longer possible, however, to rely on this tradition, because almost anything now goes as far as traditional Bavarian costume is concerned: including cowboy boots along with a miniskirt version of the dress, skullhead patterns, and Carmen-neckline blouses.

mehr verlassen, denn inzwischen ist beim Dirndl fast alles erlaubt: Cowboystiefel zum Mini-Dirndl, Totenkopfmuster auf der Tracht und Blusen mit Carmen-Ausschnitt.

Spätestens kurz vor der letzten Runde um 22.30 Uhr haben sich In- und Ausländer an den Holztischen verbrüdert. Es wird gefeiert, getanzt und manchmal auch »gebusselt«, das letzte »Noagerl« Bier wird geteilt und dann gibt es zum Abschied noch eine kleine Deutschstunde: »Ein Prosit der Gemütlichkeit«. Kurze Verschnaufpause – morgen geht es weiter.

By shortly before the last round at 10:30 p.m., at the latest, Germans and foreigners have fraternised around the wooden tables. They party, dance, and sometimes also kiss. The last sips of beer are shared, and, by way of farewell, a traditional German beer song is sung: "Ein Prosit der Gemütlichkeit". Then, after a short breather, the party continues the next day.

Schnaps Stadl
Männlich. Markant. Dreifach gebrannt.

Popcorn

BIERGARTEN

Cosby's Stagger
FELLA

Ochsenbraterei
Eisensteiner
Eisensteinerin
Werdenfelser
Isarwinkler
Tölz-Königsdorfer
Vilshofener
Festwirte Anneliese & Hermann Haberl
Antje Schneider
Warmer Leberkäs
Ochsenbraterei

LÖWENBRÄU
LÖWENBRÄU
LÖWENBRÄU
FESTWIRT
Wiggerl Hagn-Stephanie Spendler

PSCHORR
BRÄUROSL
Festwirte Georg und Renate Heide

SCHOTTENHAMEL
SPATENBRÄU

19

Bayern
Zum Bierhimmel
Boxe 18
Boxe 17
Boxe 17
Boxe 15

Deftige Wiesn-Schmankerl: Brathendl, Brezn sowie Schweinebraten mit Knödel werden gerne bestellt.
Hearty Oktoberfest fare: roast chicken, pretzels, and roast pork with dumplings are particularly popular.

Hier

Nur zum Mitnehmen
Kartoffelspalten mit Ketchup € 3.-
Chicken Wings Portion € 4.-
Schweinsbraten in der Riemischen Semmel € 4.50
Nürnberger in der Riemischen Semmel € 3.50
Fleischpflanzerl in der Riemischen Semmel € 4.-
Bitte vorher an der Kasse zahlen

SPATENBRÄU
GS
Schänke 6

Schänke
3
HB

Bei den Schankkellnern herrscht den ganzen Tag Hochbetrieb.
Bartenders are kept busy for the entire day.

HB
210

AUSSCHANK
Fischer-Vroni
Vierte Reihe.

HB

In einigen Zelten feiern bis zu 10.000 Menschen.
Some beer-tents can accommodate up to 10,000 party-goers.

SPATEN

SIMMISAMMA
HIPPODROM
Laß Dir raten

SPATEN

Rock

Für Dich

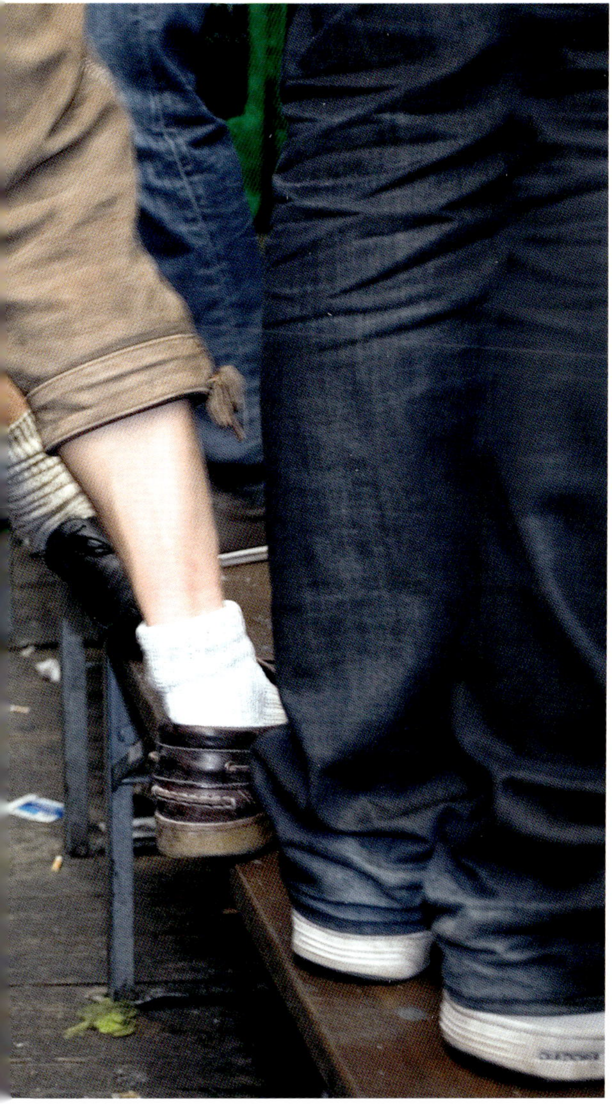

Die Bands bringen das Publikum zum Kochen.
Bands get the crowds fired up.

HB
HB
HB

W3
HIPPODROM

W5
SIMMISAMMA
Die Oktoberfestband!

Block
A B C

PAULANER

HOFBRÄU FESTZELT

Armbrustschützenzelt
PAULANER

Augustiner-Bräu

½ Wiesn'Hendl 9,25

Bei schönem Wetter sitzen die Wiesn-Besucher gerne in den Biergärten.
When the weather is fair people like to sit in the beer-gardens.

Wiesn-Besucher warten vor überfüllten Zelten.
Oktoberfest visitors wait patiently outside beer-tents that are already filled to capacity.

Die Macht des Bieres …
The power of beer …

Höher, schneller, wilder – oder doch lieber nostalgisch?

Bei den Hightech-Fahrgeschäften auf dem Oktoberfest herrscht längst ein olympischer Wettbewerbsgeist. Mit rund 100 Kilometern pro Stunde rasen Besucher in Achterbahnen durch Loopings oder lassen sich in Gondeln in alle Richtungen durch die Luft wirbeln – gute Nerven und einen guten Magen sollte man bei den hypermodernen Attraktionen schon haben.

Dabei fing alles so beschaulich an. Die Attraktionen von einst erinnern eher an einen Kindergeburtstag: Sackhüpfen, Schubkarrenrennen und Baumsteigen waren angesagt. 1818 standen ganze zwei Schaukeln und ein Karussell auf der Theresienwiese. 1881 waren es bereits 23 Schaugeschäfte, sechs Fahrgeschäfte und zwölf Schieß- und Wurfbuden. In der zweiten Hälfte des 19. Jahrhunderts kamen außerdem die Varietétheater auf. Auch das »Original-Zauber-Spezialitäten-Theater« der Künstlerfamilie Schichtl gibt es bereits seit 1869 auf dem Oktoberfest. »Auf geht's beim Schichtl«, heißt es dort jedes Jahr wieder. Während der Wiesn gibt es bis zu 30 Aufführungen täglich, bei denen Dutzende Menschen den Kopf verlieren – Freiwillige stellen sich dabei als »Enthauptungsopfer« zur Verfügung.

Von den heute rund 250 Schaustellerbetrieben haben übrigens etwa 90 Prozent ihre Wurzeln im 19. Jahrhundert. Damals wie heute ein Spaß für die

Higher, faster, wilder – or wouldn't nostalgically be better?

An Olympic spirit of competitiveness has long reigned among the high-tech fairground businesses at the Oktoberfest. Visitors loop-the-loop on rollercoasters, or fly in all directions through the air in gondolas at speeds of around 100 kilometres per hour: these hyper-modern attractions require strong nerves and a steady stomach.

But things were still very leisurely in the early days of the Oktoberfest. The attractions were then more reminiscent of a children's birthday party: sack races, wheelbarrow races, and tree-climbing were the order of the day. A total of two swings and a carousel were to be found at the Oktoberfest in 1818. By 1881, there were already 23 shows, six showground rides, and twelve shooting and tossing galleries. Variety theatres also appeared in the second half of the nineteenth century. The "Original Magic Specialities Theatre", managed by the Schichtl artists family, has also been in existence since as early as 1869. "Schichtl, here we go!" ("Auf geht's beim Schichtl") can be heard there every year. Every day at the Oktoberfest, there are up to 30 performances where dozens of people lose their heads – volunteers make themselves available as "decapitation victims".

Incidentally, around 90 percent of today's approximately 250 show business operations boast origins

ganze Familie ist das »Teufelsrad«. Seit 1910 versuchen männliche wie weibliche Besucher, sich auf der drehenden Scheibe zu halten und zugleich die Kontrahenten herunterzuschubsen. Ein »Rekommandeur« kommentiert die Leistung der Freiwilligen und erlaubt sich so manchen Spaß. »Lederhose, aus is'«, bekommt ein Bursche zu hören, der sich zu lange auf dem Rad halten kann. Dann befördert ein Schaumstoffball unter Applaus des Publikums die »Lederhose« in die gepolsterte Bande.

Dass eine Fahrt im Karussell nicht immer rasant sein muss, zeigt die »Krinoline«, die 1924 gebaut wurde. Die Höchstgeschwindigkeit beträgt ganze 15 Kilometer pro Stunde. Dieses handbemalte Karussell fährt gegen den Uhrzeigersinn und hat eine eigene Blaskapelle, die auf einem Minibalkon sitzt. Früher wurden die schwingenden Gondeln übrigens per Hand angetrieben, 1937 wurde ein elektromechanischer Antrieb eingeführt.

Wenn Männer nach dem Bierzelt-Besuch ihren Frauen oder neuen Eroberungen zeigen wollen, was für Kraftbolzen sie sind, schwingen sie auf dem Oktoberfest meist den Hammer. »Hau den Lukas« heißt das traditionelle Kräftemessen. Dabei müssen die Besucher mit einem Hammer auf einen Pflock schlagen und ein Gewicht auf einer vertikalen Säule

that stretch back to the nineteenth century. The "Teufelsrad" ("Devil's Wheel") is still an entertainment for the whole family, as in former days. Since 1910, both male and female visitors have attempted to hold on to the spinning disc, and to simultaneously push their competitors off. An announcer provides a running commentary on the volunteers' performance, while missing no opportunity to make fun of them. "Time to get off, lederhosen!", a boy, who has spent too long on the wheel, is told. Then a foam ball ejects "lederhosen" onto the padded rails, much to the audience's delight.

The "Krinoline", which was constructed in 1924, shows that a carousel ride does not always need to be hair-raising. It travels at speeds of up to no less than 15 kilometres per hour. This hand-painted carousel circulates anticlockwise, and has its own brass band seated on a miniature balcony. Incidentally, the swinging gondolas were powered by hand in earlier days, with the first electromechanical drive being deployed in 1937.

If men decide to show their wives or new conquests what musclemen they really are following a visit to the beer tents, they mostly opt for a swing of the hammer at the Oktoberfest. "Hau den Lukas" ("Smack Lucas") is the name of the traditional

nach oben schnellen lassen. Viele im Fitnessstudio gestählte Burschen schwanken zur Belustigung der Zuschauer schon, wenn sie den schweren Hammer nur hochheben, und enden auf der Kräfteskala gar als »Schlappschwanz«. So manch

schmächtiger Jüngling stellt sich wiederum als wahrer Herkules heraus. Wenn das Gewicht bis ganz nach oben schnellt, ertönt eine Klingel. Der Beifall der Umstehenden ist dem »Weltmeister« dann sicher – und das zählt viel mehr als der eigentliche Preis, eine Tröte oder eine Plastikrose.

Für die »richtigen« Männer gibt es auch noch den »Toboggan«. 1908 standen drei Exemplare dieser Riesenrutschbahn auf der Wiesn. Mittels eines Förderbands werden die Fahrgäste etwa die Hälfte des Aufstiegs nach oben transportiert. Der Handlauf bewegt sich, anders als bei einer Rolltreppe, nicht mit. Wer sich daran festhalten will, den haut es auf den Allerwertesten. Während Frauen bei der kurzen Fahrt von charmanten Helfern die Hand gereicht bekommen, versuchen die Männer, die paar Meter auf dem Förderband selbst zu bewältigen – was nicht immer gelingt. Von der Turmspitze aus rutscht man in einer sich um den Turm windenden Holzrinne nach unten.

strength-testing game. Here, visitors strike a post with a hammer, and a weight shoots up a vertical pillar. To the amusement of the onlookers, many gym-honed young men start to totter and sway as soon as they lift the hammer, before the strength-meter categorises them as "wimps". Whereas many a slightly built youth turns out to be a genuine Hercules. A bell rings if the weight darts all the way to the top. The "World Champion" is then sure of the audience's applause – which is worth much more than the actual prize: a horn, or a plastic rose.

For "real men", there is still the "Toboggan". There were three versions of this huge slide on the Oktoberfest grounds in 1908. A conveyor belt draws passengers about half the way to the top. By contrast with an escalator, the handrail does not move along with the conveyor belt. Passengers who try to hold on to it receive a blow to the posterior. While women can count on helping hands from charming helpers during the short ride, men attempt the few meters on the conveyor belts by themselves – which doesn't always work. The slide consists of a wooden channel that winds around the tower from top to bottom.

Kinder und Erwachsene staunen beim »Floh-Circus« (Bild oben). Die kleinen Artisten, weibliche Tierflöhe, sind an Golddrähten befestigt und führen kleine Kunststücke vor. Sie schießen Bälle, drehen ein Karussell, das viel schwerer ist als sie selbst, oder sie ziehen eine Kutsche. Alle paar Stunden müssen die Flöhe gefüttert werden, dafür setzt der Dompteur die Tiere auf seinen Unterarm.

Ebenfalls ein Vergnügen für die ganze Familie ist das 50 Meter hohe »Riesenrad«. Vom höchsten Punkt aus kann man die ganze Theresienwiese überblicken. Bei Föhn, bei dem die Sicht besonders gut ist, scheinen die Berge zum Greifen nah zu sein. Und einer darf auf der Wiesn natürlich nicht fehlen: der Münchner »Vogeljakob« (Bild oben rechts). Seine kleine Holzbude ist immer von einer Menschentraube umringt, die dem Zirpen und Zwitschern lauscht. Das kleine »Pfeiferl« muss auf der Zunge liegen, bis der Papierteil weich ist. Danach drückt man es an den Gaumen und spricht bei

Children and adults marvel at the "Floh-Circus" ("flea circus", picture left). The tiny artistes, female animal-fleas, are secured to the gold wires, and perform little tricks. They hit balls, turn a carousel around that is much heavier than they are, or they draw a carriage. Every few hours, the flea-trainer feeds the animals by placing them on his forearm. The 50-meter high "Riesenrad" ("Big Wheel") is another fun attraction for the whole family. The top of the wheel affords a view of the entire Oktoberfest grounds. When the visibility is particularly good during "Foehn wind" conditions, it seems almost possible to reach out and touch the mountains in the distance.

Munich's "Vogeljakob" ("Bird-man", picture top) is another attraction that should never be missing at the Oktoberfest. There is always a cluster of people around his small wooden stall listening to his chirping and tweeting. The small pipe must rest on your tongue until its paper part softens. Then it

geschlossenen Zähnen »sch, tsch, tschiro oder tschrü …« – ob das allerdings nach zwei Maß Bier auch noch funktioniert, sollten Sie besser selbst probieren.

Und dann – kaum hat die Wiesn begonnen, ist sie schon wieder vorbei. Am letzten Wochenende sind die meisten Touristen schon abgereist und die Einheimischen fast wieder unter sich. Es wird eine letzte Runde bestellt, ein letztes Mal geschunkelt und mit Sternwerfern oder Leuchtstäben in der Hand ein letztes Mal aus voller Kehle gesungen. Bedienungen liegen sich in den Armen. Es wird gelacht, es wird geweint, es heißt Abschied nehmen – bis zum nächsten Jahr.

is pressed against the gums, and, through closed teeth, sounds such as "tweet tweet, chirp chirp" and similar are produced – now, whether this works after two litres of beer or not, is something you should try for yourself.

And then, it seems that – the Oktoberfest has only just begun – when it's already over. Most of the tourists have already departed by the last weekend, leaving the citizens of Munich almost to themselves. A last round is ordered, the crowd sways to the music for one last time, clutching sparklers and glow sticks, and singing from the tops of their voices. Waiters and waitresses stand arm-in-arm. And then laughter, tears, and farewells – until next year.

Pschorr-Bräurosl
AUGUSTINER BRÄU

Vorhergehende Doppelseite:
Blick von der Paulskirche auf die Theresienwiese
View of the Theresienwiese from the Paulskirche

Rechte Seite:
Unter all den Fahrgeschäften ist das Riesenrad bei den Besuchern nach wie vor besonders beliebt: In 50 Metern Höhe ist die Aussicht am schönsten.
The Big Wheel, of all the fairground rides, remains a particular attraction among visitors: it offers the best view from an altitude of 50 metres.

Willenborg
Eingang
SPATEN

DUNLOP SPEZIAL
Nächste Vorstellung
NEXT SHOW

ALPINA BAHN

R
C
Wellenflug
Circus Welt

50 Jahre
KASS

NYMPHENBURG SEKT
10

Bratwurst gehört genauso zur Wiesn wie türkischer Honig, Lebkuchenherzen, gebrannte Mandeln und Steckerlfisch.
Bratwurst is just as much a part of the Oktoberfest as Turkish honey, gingerbread hearts, roast almonds and fish on a stick.

TECHNO

06
My bear

EINMAL
los abgeräumt
3Bälle 2.- €

PAULANER
HB
MÜNCHEN

Käfer
Käfer Wiesn Schänke

MÜNCHEN

Playball
Playball

Pschorr-Bräurosl
CUS

Franziskaner

Ausklang mit Wunderkerzen am letzten Wiesn-Abend
Sparklers are popular with visitors as the final Oktoberfest evening draws to a close.

Manch Besucher schläft auf dem Heimweg schon in der U-Bahn ein.
Many visitors are already asleep on the subway on their way home.

AMMER

terra magica

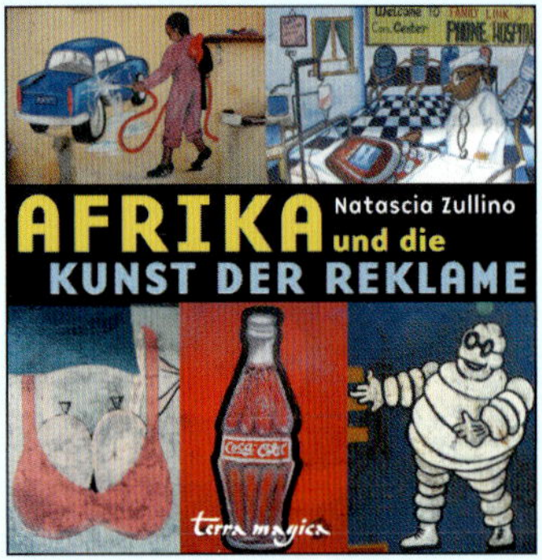

120 Seiten mit 182 Fotos
ISBN 978-3-7243-1021-1

Werbung mal ganz anders!

120 Seiten mit ca. 100 Fotos
ISBN 978-3-7243-1017-4

Ein atmosphärisches Porträt der Tango-Metropole …

120 Seiten mit ca. 100 Fotos
ISBN 978-3-7243-1026-6

Stubentiger zum Verlieben …

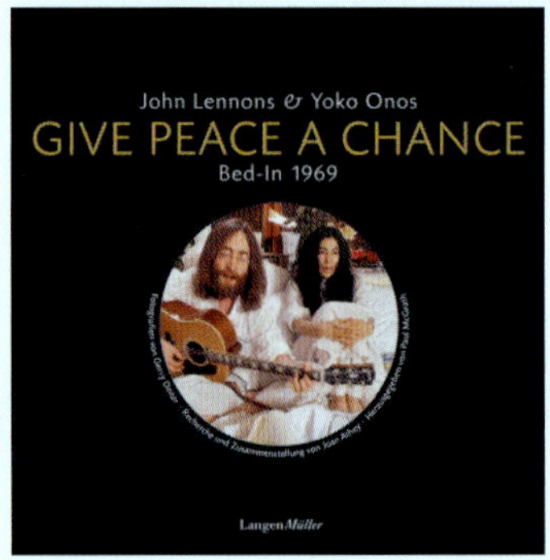

104 Seiten mitca. 80 Fotos
ISBN 978-3-7844-3186-4

Das legendäre Bed-In 1969.

Satz: Birgit Veits
Reproduktionen: Gerber KG/Tausend Verlagsservice
Printed in EU
ISBN 978-3-7243-1025-9

Besuchen Sie uns im Internet unter www.terramagica.de

vom Münchner
Oktoberfest
möchte mit
Schön, dass es Dich gibt
Mein schlägt nur für Dich
Wolke 7
Weil ich Dich
Heute
single